THE LIBRARY OF

nutrition™

Planning and Preparing Healthy Meals and Snacks

A Day-to-Day Guide to a Healthier Diet

Jennifer Silate

New York

Published in 2005, 2008 by The Rosen Publishing Company, Inc.
29 East 21st Street, New York, NY 10010

Revised Edition, 2008

Library of Congress Cataloging-in-Publication Data

Silate, Jennifer.
Planning and preparing healthy meals and snacks : a day-to-day guide to a healthier diet / by Jennifer Silate.— 1st ed.
p. cm. — (The Library of nutrition)
Includes bibliographical references and index.
ISBN 978-1-4042-1870-3 (library binding)
ISBN 978-1-4042-1634-1 (paperback)
6-Pack ISBN 978-1-4042-1638-9
1. Menus—Juvenile literature. 2. Cookery—Planning—Juvenile literature.
3. Snack foods—Juvenile literature. 4. Nutrition—Juvenile literature.
I. Title. II. Series.
TX728.S57 2005
642'.4—dc22

2004015540

Manufactured in the United States of America

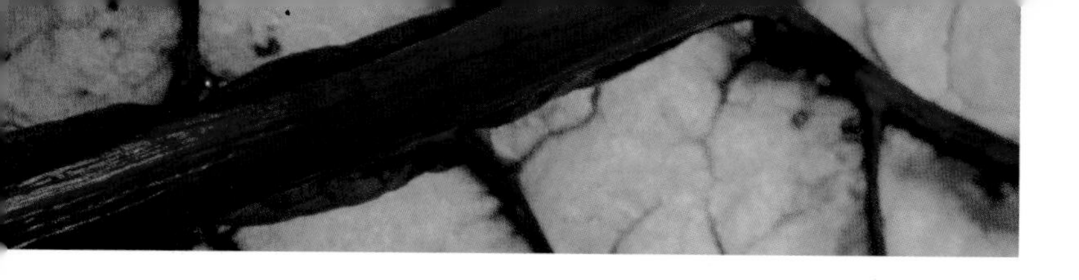

contents

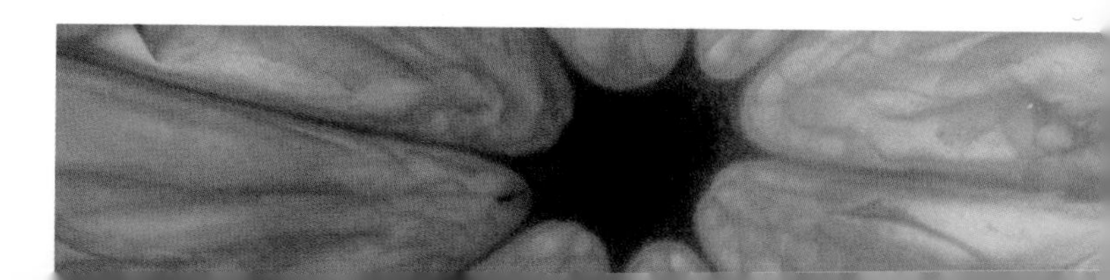

introduction

What did you eat today? Did you have a doughnut for breakfast or a bowl of whole-grain cereal? What fruits and vegetables did you eat? You already know that you need to eat fruits, vegetables, grains, and other nutritious foods to stay healthy, but how much of each should you eat?

With each meal of each day, you are presented with an array of food options that vary widely in their nutritional value. Today, unfortunately, many people have an unbalanced diet that features too many carbohydrates and fats. In our hectic society, people save time that they would otherwise spend cooking a nutritious meal by eating out at fast-food restaurants or buying frozen dinners. Most of these quick alternatives are unhealthy and fattening.

For example, at lunch, many people take the fast-food route and have a hamburger and french fries, instead of opting for a more nutritious, less fattening meal. If you tend to be one of the people who always chooses the hamburger, chances are your body is lacking some essential nutrients it needs to stay healthy. Cookies, ice cream, candy bars, and potato chips may taste good and satisfy your hunger for a little while, but they are not nutritious snacks. Sugary snacks provide jolts of energy that are

While pizza is a quick and easy meal that can contain nutritious tomato sauce and other vegetables, it can also be high in fat and sodium, depending on the toppings. If pizza is a regular part of your diet, try making it at home from wholesome ingredients.

quickly spent. You will probably be hungry again a short while after eating them. In addition, if sweets are consumed in excess, they are stored as fat. Healthy foods provide your body with more steady and sustained energy that will carry you to your next meal.

To become healthy, you must change your eating habits and learn which foods are good for you and which are not. You must eat well-balanced meals—featuring fruits, vegetables, whole grains, and the proper proportions of fats, carbohydrates, and proteins—and exercise for thirty minutes at least five times each week. Learning about nutrition, taking control of your eating habits, and exercising will help you

A great way to begin creating a healthier diet is to take part in your family's grocery shopping. If you help with the shopping, you can choose nutritious food that will make healthy meals and snacks.

strengthen your body and boost your energy. When you learn about good nutrition, you gain the tools you need to make healthy food decisions. You learn what vitamins and nutrients your body needs in a day and exactly how and where to get them. Achieving good health is not only beneficial for your growing body, it also safeguards your bones and muscles for years to come. Small changes in your diet now can reduce your risk for illness and disease later in life.

It is easier than you think to prepare healthy meals and snacks. There are many food options that are not only nutritious, but also delicious. Read on to learn about how to plan and prepare healthy meals and snacks that will give you the energy and nutrients your body needs, while satisfying your craving for tasty foods.

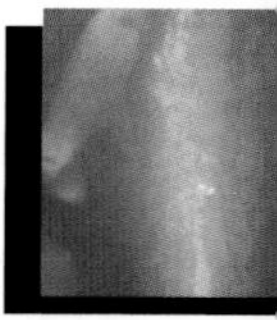
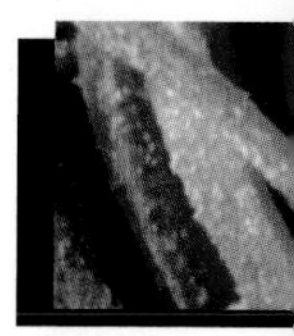
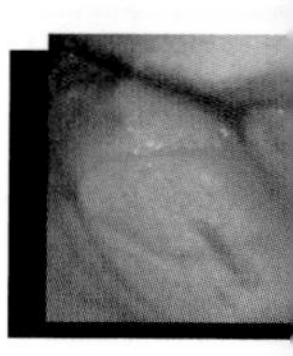

chapter 1

MyPyramid and You

Americans have access to a wide variety of foods. It can be hard to decide which are the healthiest. Having so many choices can be confusing. After purchasing groceries, you must plan how to use these foods to create nutritious meals.

The United States Department of Agriculture (USDA) developed the MyPyramid food plan to help people create a healthy, balanced diet. MyPyramid differs from previous food pyramids, which organized food groups in rows and emphasized numbers of servings. On the MyPyramid symbol, a person climbing steps stresses the importance of physical activity. The six bands of color stand for six food categories: grains, vegetables, fruits, oils, milk, and meat and beans. The bands' different widths show that people should eat more from some groups than others. Each band's wide bottom stands for foods with little or no solid fats or added sugar. You should eat these foods more than foods that contain more solid fats and added sugar (represented by the band's narrow top).

Each individual needs their own nutrition and exercise plan. MyPyramid.gov is a Web site that can help you figure

Each band of the MyPyramid symbol represents a food category: grains (orange); vegetables (green); fruits (red); oils (yellow); milk (blue); meats and beans (purple).

out what your personal plan should be. It can guide you in making better choices and creating a balance between food and physical activity.

Grains

The orange band on the left side represents the grain group. This includes cereals, breads, crackers, rice, and pasta. These foods provide carbohydrates, your body's main source of energy. Carbohydrates may be simple or complex. Simple carbohydrates are found in sugar and sweets. They are easily absorbed by the body and cause your blood sugar level to rise and fall quickly. This gives you a short burst of energy but then leaves you tired and hungry. Complex carbohydrates are found in rice, pasta, cereal, bread, and crackers. They are absorbed more slowly than simple carbohydrates and help maintain steady blood sugar levels, giving you energy for a longer time.

The USDA recommends that you eat at least 6 ounces of grains daily. (One ounce is about 1 slice of bread, 1 cup of cereal, or 1/2 cup of cooked rice, cereal, or pasta.) At least half your daily grains should be whole grains. They have more fiber, vitamins, and minerals than refined grains. Evidence suggests that a high-fiber diet may lower the risk of some types of cancer.

Vegetables

The green band is the vegetable group. The USDA recommends you eat 2 1/2 cups of vegetables daily. Vegetables provide a variety of vitamins and minerals. For example, broccoli and spinach provide vitamin A, vitamin C, iron, and more. Vitamin A plays an important part in vision, fighting infection, and regulating the immune system. Vitamin C helps the body fight infection and stimulates the immune system. Red blood

Fruits, vegetables, and nuts like the ones shown here provide a colorful, flavorful, and nutritious spark to your diet and boost your energy level.

cells use iron to carry oxygen throughout the body.

It's a good idea to eat different kinds of vegetables so your body gets a variety of vitamins and minerals. The USDA recommends dark leafy greens such as spinach, orange vegetables such as sweet potatoes, and dry beans such as lentils.

Fruits

The red band represents the fruit group. Most fruits are a good source of vitamins A and C, as well as fiber and potassium. Potassium is an important mineral that assists in muscle contraction and in maintaining the balance of fluid in body cells. It's also involved in sending nerve impulses and releasing energy from protein, fat, and carbohydrates in food.

The USDA recommends eating 1 1/2 cups of fruit daily. By eating a variety of fruit, you can be sure to get a wide range of vitamins. Although you can eat fresh, frozen, canned, or dried fruit or even drink fruit juice, be aware that some canned fruit and fruit juices have added sugar and lack fiber. Fresh fruit is often the most nutritious option.

Oils

The thin yellow strip is the oils group. Oils are fats that are liquid at room temperature. They come from plants and fish. Common oils include canola oil, olive oil, and peanut oil. The USDA recommends that you eat only a small amount of foods high in fats.

There are several types of fat: saturated fat, trans fat, monounsaturated fat, and polyunsaturated fat. Saturated fat (found in whole milk, red meat, and butter) and trans fat (found in margarine, shortening, fried foods, and many snack foods) are unhealthy fats. They boost cholesterol, clog arteries, and cause heart disease, strokes, and other health problems. Limiting these fats in your diet is a good way to keep your heart healthy. Monounsaturated and polyunsaturated fats are found in nuts, fish, and vegetable oils. Research has shown that these fats are actually good for your heart and may reduce blood cholesterol levels.

Children from nine to thirteen years old are recommended to have about 5 teaspoons of oil each day. Two tablespoons of peanut butter contain about 4 teaspoons of oil. MyPyramid.gov can help you find out how much oil is in foods you like to eat.

Milk

The blue band is the milk group. Dairy foods such as milk, yogurt, and cheese give your body calcium, which helps make bones and teeth strong. The USDA recommends that people over the age of eight have 3 cups of dairy daily. Up until you are about thirty years old, the body stores calcium for the future. As you get older, you begin to lose bone density. Your bones become brittle and break more easily. Stored calcium helps slow bone loss and keep the bones as strong as possible for as long as possible.

Unfortunately, dairy foods are often high in fat. When choosing your daily dairy foods, you should limit the amount of high-fat cheeses and desserts you eat and select more low-fat dairy products, such as skim milk, nonfat or low-fat yogurt, and small amounts of hard cheeses.

Meat and Beans

The purple band represents the meat and beans group. This group contains protein-rich foods such as meat, poultry, fish, beans, eggs, nuts, and seeds. Protein is an important part of your diet. Your body uses it to help develop muscle, carry vitamins through your bloodstream, build new cells, and maintain tissues. About 5 ounces of protein are recommended daily. One small hamburger is about 2 or 3 ounces of protein.

Some forms of protein are healthier than others. Red meat is among the most popular protein sources but also among the least healthy. It's high in fat and can be high in cholesterol, which can clog your arteries. Low-fat meats and poultry are better choices. Fish, nuts, and seeds contain healthy oils that may help fight heart disease and provide other health benefits. Vary your protein choices, but try to choose lean when possible.

FACT!

Eating only a few calories a day can actually make you gain weight. When your body receives a small amount of food during the day, it slows down its metabolism, the rate at which food is used by the body. When you start eating normally again, food will be stored as fat until your metabolism returns to its normal level.

This is a microscopic image of a blood vessel whose lining is clogged with cholesterol and other fatty deposits. These deposits are the red substance. The passage through which blood and oxygen flow (the white area at the vessel's center) has become very narrow, restricting the flow of blood and oxygen to the heart. This disorder, known as atherosclerosis, can lead to coronary heart disease and strokes.

Calorie Choices and Physical Activity

MyPyramid suggests that only a small number of calories each day come from foods containing solid fats, such as butter or shortening, or sugar, such as candy or soda. A calorie is a measure of how much energy a food will give you. Check MyPyramid.gov to see how many calories you need each day. The USDA calls solid fats and sugars "discretionary calories" because you should use discretion, or good judgment, about eating them. If a person needs around 2,000 calories each day, a little over 1,700 calories are needed for essential nutrients from the other food groups. This leaves fewer than 300 discretionary calories. How

A Nebraska teenager suffering from anorexia nervosa stands in her bedroom as her concerned father looks in.

much is this? One cup of vanilla ice cream contains about 205 discretionary calories. High-calorie foods such as cookies and sodas often have little nutritional value. Use the information on food labels to help you keep track of the calories, fat, and sugar you eat each day.

If a person consumes more calories daily than they burn off, they will gain weight. The climbing figure on MyPyramid reminds us that physical activity should include at least thirty minutes of moderate exercise (such as walking or bicycling) or vigorous exercise (such as running or swimming) five days a week. Increasing your heart rate has proven benefits for your body and can help you lose or maintain weight.

Beware of becoming too focused on weight and calorie counting. The desire to become thin can become obsessive and lead to dangerous eating disorders, such as anorexia and bulimia nervosa. Teenagers need enough nutrients in the day to keep their bodies strong and healthy as they finish growing into adulthood. Starving yourself or allowing yourself to eat only a small number of calories each day can stunt your growth and lead to serious health problems. A healthy diet is one in which you don't feel hungry all the time or uncomfortably full after each meal. A variety of wholesome foods will keep your body energized and strong.

chapter 2

Daily Meal Strategies

Now that we know about MyPyramid and its elements, the next important step is putting its recommendations into practice in our daily lives. Following guidelines may seem difficult at first, but with a little knowledge, planning, and practice, you will soon have no problem planning and preparing healthy meals and snacks.

Getting the Facts Straight

In 1990, the U.S. government passed a law that required most packaged foods (as well as some raw and restaurant-prepared foods) to bear a Nutrition Facts label. This standardized label lists how much of several different nutrients—including fat, cholesterol, sodium, carbohydrates, protein, vitamins, and minerals—a single serving of the food contains. It also lists what percentage of the daily recommended totals of those nutrients is provided in a single serving. This label should be used as a guide to help you determine where in your diet the food fits and how much of it you should have.

Try to familiarize yourself with the nutrition facts of some of your favorite foods so that you know how often and how much of that food you should be eating to stay healthy.

Nutrition Facts
Serving Size 1 patty (71g)
Servings Per Container 4

Amount Per Serving	
Calories 110	Calories from Fat 45
	% **Daily Value***
Total Fat 5g	**8%**
Saturated Fat 0.5g	**3%**
Trans Fat 0g	
Cholesterol 0mg	**0%**
Sodium 380mg	**16%**
Total Carbohydrate 6g	**2%**
Dietary Fiber 4g	**15%**
Sugars 0g	
Protein 12g	

Vitamin A 2% • Vitamin C 0%
Calcium 8% • Iron 8%

*Percent Daily Values are based on a 2,000 calorie diet. Your daily values may be higher or lower depending on your calorie needs:

	Calories:	2,000	2,500
Total Fat	Less than	65g	80g
Sat Fat	Less than	20g	25g
Cholesterol	Less than	300mg	300mg
Sodium	Less than	2,400mg	2,400mg
Total Carbohydrate		300g	375g
Dietary Fiber		25g	30g

Calories per gram:
Fat 9 • Carbohydrate 4 • Protein 4

The Nutrition Facts panel that appears on nearly all packaged foods and drinks offers a wealth of information on the product's nutritional value. By learning how to understand the panel, you can determine how any given food or drink item fits into your daily dietary needs.

How Many Meals per Day?

There has been some debate over whether people should eat three large meals each day or five or six smaller ones. Studies have shown that eating several small meals throughout the day helps your body burn fat faster by giving it a steady supply of energy. Eating bigger meals only three times a day creates peaks and valleys of energy. Many people, however, do not have the time in their busy schedule to eat six small meals each day. Snacking can be a way to keep your body energized between meals. Try keeping healthy snacks in easy-to-reach places, such as your book bag or purse. Some options for snacks are carrot sticks, a small box of raisins, low-fat trail mix, granola bars, or a piece of fruit. If healthy snacks are on hand, you will be less tempted by junk food.

Getting a Good Start

When you wake up in the morning, your body needs fuel to become physically active and mentally alert. A nutritious breakfast gives your body the nutrients and energy it needs to start the day. Sugary cereals and pastries that are high in calories will give your body a quick boost of energy but leave you feeling tired well before lunchtime. A good choice in the morning would be a breakfast cereal with bran, wheat, or other nutritious grains and low-fat or skim milk. Many cereals today are also fortified with vitamins and minerals in order to really pack a nutritious punch. Low-fat fruit yogurt with granola and fruit is another good breakfast option. It gives you dairy, fruit, and grains to start your day.

What to Munch at Lunch

Today, school cafeterias offer a variety of lunch foods that are more nutritious than the heavy, fried, and starchy meals of past years. Yet many schools still offer meals that are high in sugar, fat, and sodium. When choosing what to have for lunch, think about what you had for breakfast and then determine what gaps in MyPyramid you need to fill. If you have a choice between a fried fish sandwich and a grilled chicken sandwich, the grilled chicken sandwich would be the better choice. Like the fish, it offers protein, but because it is grilled rather than fried, it is much lower in fat.

If you bring your lunch to school, you will have more control over what you are eating. When preparing your lunch, beware of extra fat and calories lurking in the condiments you choose, such as ketchup, mayonnaise, and salad dressing. Mustard is a healthier choice than mayonnaise for sandwiches. It has no fat and 3 to 15 calories, while mayonnaise has about eleven grams of fat and 100 calories per tablespoon.

Two hikers take a snack break by sharing a bag of trail mix. Trail mix, usually made with nuts, raisins, seeds, and perhaps granola or chocolate bits, is a high-protein, vitamin-rich treat that provides quick but sustained energy.

Snack Time

When you get home from school, there are probably a few hours left until dinnertime. A healthy snack can keep your energy levels up and prevent feelings of hunger between meals. In fact, snacking can be an important part of your diet and a great opportunity to fulfill some of the recommendations of MyPyramid. When deciding what you want for a snack, think about what you had for breakfast or lunch. Did you have 2 cups of fruit but no vegetables? If you did, you might want to have some carrot sticks. If you only had 1 cup of dairy, you may want to have a piece of string cheese or a cup of low-fat yogurt as a snack. These snacks will keep you healthy and satisfied without adding unwanted weight. They will actually make it easier for you to maintain your ideal weight. Those who do not snack tend to binge on large meals, while those who snack on junk food that contains few, if any, nutrients end up consuming lots of empty calories, sugar, sodium, and fat.

FACT!

A can of soda contains almost ten teaspoons of sugar on average.

The lunches sold at this school are of the high-fat, high-calorie, low-nutrient variety, including cheeseburgers, french fries, and breaded and fried chicken patties. Whenever possible, avoid these kinds of fried and fatty offerings and opt instead for leafy salads, veggie or lean-meat sandwiches, and fruit salads.

Be a Winner at Dinner

When dinnertime arrives, you should again think about what you had to eat that day. Try to fill any remaining gaps in MyPyramid's recommendations. Also, keep an eye on your serving sizes. A heaping plate full of pasta could easily represent 4 ounces of grains. When you are the one preparing the meal, use olive oil, sesame oil, or nonstick spray to grease pans and cook foods rather than the saturated fat, high-cholesterol alternatives of butter or lard (beef shortening).

If you go out to eat, try to avoid fried foods and creamy or cheesy sauces. These foods are high in fat and calories. Meats should be grilled,

A variety of tasty and colorful vegetables stir-fried in a small amount of olive or canola oil and served over brown rice is a quick, easy meal that is also delicious and nutritious.

broiled, or baked rather than fried. Dishes should be served with a variety of raw, stir-fried, or grilled vegetables. A good rule of thumb is that the more colorful the meal, the more nutrients you will be getting, so look for lots of red, green, orange, and yellow vegetables. Believe it or not, nutritious meals can even be found at fast-food restaurants these days. Most now offer grilled chicken sandwiches and fresh garden salads, yogurt, fruit, and whole-grain bread and rolls.

Each dinner can be a success if, before preparing or ordering it, you stop to think about what you have already eaten that day and what food groups and nutrients you still need to cover. If you do not get the recommended amount of a given food group one day, do not worry. You can always try to make up the difference the next day by giving that food group or nutrient extra emphasis. The inverse is also true; if you overdo it on sweets or fatty foods one day, simply limit the sweets and fatty foods you eat in the next few meals. A little planning and discipline will help keep you happy and healthy.

chapter 3

Food Safety

Nutrition is an important part of staying healthy, but handling your food safely is just as important to your physical health. Before you prepare a meal, it is important that you know how to handle food so that you and those who eat your food stay safe. According to the USDA, more than 76 million Americans suffer from a foodborne illness every year. The National Center for Health Statistics estimates that 9,100 Americans die from food poisoning each year. You can greatly reduce your chances of contracting a foodborne illness if you follow some basic rules when handling food.

Storage Safety

Safe food handling starts in the grocery store. When you go shopping for food, be sure to keep raw meat and poultry away from other food. Sometimes, the packages that raw meats are kept in can leak. The liquid that leaks from the package contains bacteria that could contaminate other foods it comes into contact with, such as unpackaged fruits and vegetables. Also make sure that any cans you buy are not dented. Dented cans may contain small holes through which bacteria can enter. Try to buy perishable foods—such

as milk, meat, and eggs—toward the end of your shopping trip so that they are kept refrigerated for the longest time possible and bacteria does not have a chance to start to grow.

When you get home from the grocery store, refrigerate the perishables immediately. It is best to keep eggs, milk, and meat inside the body of the refrigerator rather than on one of its door shelves. This is because the temperature of the door shelves is always rising and dropping when the door is opened and closed. The temperature inside the main body of the refrigerator remains more constant. Different foods can last for different amounts of time when refrigerated. Milk and eggs have expiration dates on their cartons, which you should check when buying the products and before using them. Fruits can last for three to seven days before they go bad. Uncooked meats should only be kept for two to five days in the refrigerator, but they can be frozen up to four to twelve months. Poultry should only be kept refrigerated for two days. If any refrigerated meat looks or smells bad, it probably is, so don't eat it.

Perishable items should be refrigerated as soon as you return from the grocery store, with the most temperature-sensitive items—such as milk, eggs, meat, and poultry—placed far back on the refrigerator's shelves.

Freezing breads and meats allows you to keep them for months instead of days. Care must be taken, however, to make sure that food is not thawed and

then refrozen. Meats and other foods that have been frozen, thawed, and refrozen can contain harmful bacteria that can lead to food poisoning. The only food that can safely be frozen more than once is bread. Defrosting should always be done either in the refrigerator, the microwave, or in a sink under cold running water (for meats). Never leave meat out on the counter to defrost. Leaving meat at room temperature for long periods of time is an open invitation for bacteria.

It is extremely important to wash your hands before, during, and after preparing food and before eating. Germs can be passed from unclean hands to food, usually when the food handler does not wash after using the toilet. The germs are then passed on to those who eat the food. Germs can also spread from raw, uncooked foods, such as chicken or hamburger, to the hands, then from the hands to other foods, such as salad.

Food Preparation

When you are ready to cook your meal, it is important to remember to handle food safely. Always wash your hands with soap and hot water for at least twenty seconds before handling food. Make sure that your knives, cutting boards, and any other utensils that you plan to use when preparing your meal are also clean.

Raw meats and other foods can carry many forms of bacteria that can make you sick if you're not careful. Salmonella—a poisonous bacteria found in undercooked poultry,

Salmonella bacteria grow in this petri dish. Infection with the bacteria can cause diarrhea, fever, and abdominal cramps for four to seven days. Most people recover without treatment, but some require hospitalization. People become infected with the bacteria by eating foods contaminated with solid animal waste introduced by food handlers who have not washed their hands. Any kind of food can become contaminated and still look and smell normal.

meat, seafood, and eggs—is the leading cause of death from foodborne illness. The U.S. Food and Drug Administration (FDA) notes there are more than 40,000 cases of salmonella poisoning reported in America each year. Salmonella easily spreads from food to food and can be found on fruit, vegetables, and other foods that have come into contact with the bacteria. If possible, you should use two cutting boards when preparing a meal: one for raw meats and another for fruits and vegetables. This will ensure that bacteria from the meats doesn't spread to your other food. After handling raw meat, it's important to use soap and hot water to wash every utensil and surface that came into contact with it. This will kill any bacteria that might be lingering on knives, cutting boards, or your hands.

When preparing meats, a meat thermometer will help you determine when they're fully cooked. Roasts and steaks should reach 145° Fahrenheit (63°C), ground beef should reach 160° Fahrenheit (71°C), and poultry should be cooked until it reaches 180° Fahrenheit (82°C). At these temperatures, bacteria cannot survive. To check the temperature of a piece of meat or poultry, stick the thermometer into the thickest part of the meat. This is the portion of the meat that is the slowest to cook. Eggs should be cooked until the yolk and white are firm, not runny.

FACT!

Your refrigerator should be set to 40° Fahrenheit (4°C) or below and the freezer set to 0° Fahrenheit (-18°C) in order to prevent bacteria from developing on your foods.

Concerns about food safety in the kitchen should not stop once the food has been cooked. If there are leftovers, you will need to store them in the refrigerator. Many people like to relax and watch television, read a book, or play games after a meal. Before you do so, however, make sure that your leftovers are put away. Food should not be left at room temperature for more than two hours. If you have a lot of leftovers, it is best to divide them into a few small containers rather than one big one so that they will cool faster. Warm temperatures encourage the growth of dangerous bacteria. Rapid refrigeration will ensure that your leftovers will be safe to eat later. If you do not think that you will eat the leftovers in the next two to three days, it is best to put them in the freezer rather than the refrigerator. Bacteria cannot grow in subfreezing temperatures, so your food will keep for a lot longer. Ensuring the safety of the food you eat is a major part of eating well and staying healthy.

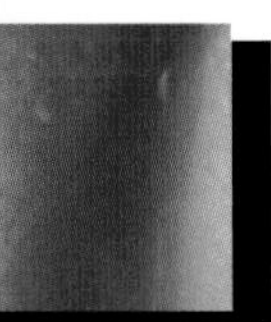

chapter 4

A Five-Day Healthy Meal Plan

A healthy diet does not have to be boring, bland, or unappetizing. Many nutritious dishes also happen to be delicious. What follows is a meal plan that includes five days' worth of menus for nutritious meals and snacks. In order to get a good start on your new and healthier lifestyle, try to follow this example, making substitutions based on your preferences. After the five days, you will probably begin to get the hang of planning healthy meals, and you will better understand the basic elements of nutritious foods. You will then be able to begin devising your own meal plans along similar lines to this one. After a few weeks, you will probably find the unhealthy foods you used to eat less tempting than they once were. You may be surprised by just how good nutritious food can taste.

Day 1

Breakfast

1 c. low-fat yogurt
1/2 c. almond granola
1 c. orange juice

Lunch

Tuna Fish Sandwich
2 oz. tuna fish
1 tbsp. low-fat mayonnaise
1 lettuce leaf
2 tomato slices
2 slices whole-wheat bread
7–8 carrot sticks
1/2 c. unsalted pretzels
1 c. skim milk

Snack

3 c. popcorn, popped

Using an air popper is the healthiest way to make popcorn. If you do not have an air popper, choose natural or plain microwavable popcorn instead of butter flavored. Flavored popcorns are usually high in fat and calories. For extra flavor on plain popcorn, sprinkle two teaspoons of grated Parmesan cheese or paprika over it. These are low-fat, tasty alternatives to butter or salt.

Unsalted, unflavored air-popped popcorn can make a satisfying, tasty snack that is high in fiber and carbohydrates and low in fat and calories.

Dinner

Recipe: PERSONAL PIZZAS

These do-it-yourself pizzas are a more nutritious alternative to either pizzeria-style or frozen pizzas.

Ingredients

1 small whole-wheat pita or tortilla
2 tbsp. pizza sauce
1/3 c. low-fat mozzarella cheese
2–3 oz. diced chicken
1 c. of your favorite vegetables—mushrooms, peppers, onions, tomatoes, and broccoli are all good choices—cut into slices

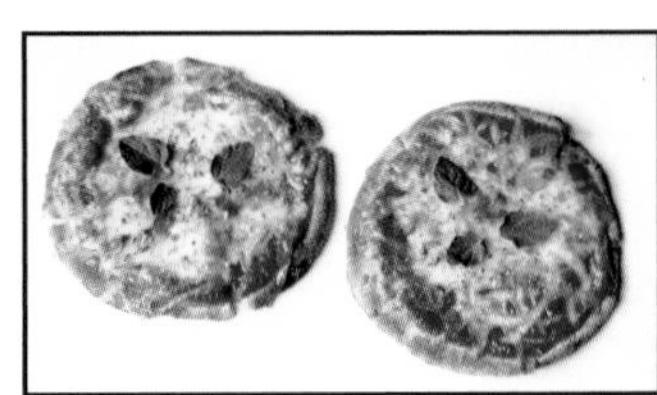

Directions: Preheat oven to 350° Fahrenheit (177°C). Place pita or tortilla on cookie sheet; this will be your crust. Spread pizza sauce over crust. Sprinkle cheese on top of sauce. Place vegetables and chicken on top of cheese. Bake in oven for about fifteen minutes, until cheese is bubbly and vegetables are cooked. Allow to cool for several minutes before eating.

Dessert

3–4 tbsp. fruit salad over a small piece of angel food cake

The meal plan for day one features a variety of food selections. Six ounces of grain servings include granola, whole-wheat bread, pretzels, popcorn, pita pizza crust, and angel food cake. The orange juice and fruit salad provide about 1 1/2 cups of fruit. The carrot sticks from lunch and toppings

on the pizza provide about 2 1/2 cups of vegetables. Also, yogurt, milk, and cheese from the pizza provide 3 cups of dairy. Finally, protein is provided by nuts in the granola, tuna fish, and chicken on the pizza. Notice that this menu provides a limited amount of fat and sugar.

Day 2

Breakfast

1 c. cereal
1/4 c. skim milk
1 banana
1/2 c. orange juice

Lunch

Chef's Salad
1 c. romaine lettuce
2–3 oz. ham and turkey
1 large tomato, chopped
1 carrot, sliced
1 cucumber, sliced
1 hard-boiled egg
1/4 c. cheddar cheese, shredded
croutons
2 tbsp. olive oil–and–vinegar dressing
1 whole-wheat roll
1 c. skim milk

A chef's salad can provide you with a significant source of your day's nutritional requirements, including vegetables, protein (turkey and ham), and dairy (grated cheese).

Snack

1–2 oz. cheddar cheese
6 wheat crackers
1 apple

Dinner

4 oz. barbecued grilled chicken breast
1/2 c. green beans
1 c. cooked brown rice

Today's menu fulfills many requirements of the MyPyramid food plan. Salads are a good way to eat a variety of foods, including several cups of vegetables, in a single meal. This menu also includes whole grains: a whole-wheat roll, wheat crackers, and brown rice. Substituting whole grains for refined grains is a good way of providing your body with more fiber, vitamins, and minerals.

Day 3

Breakfast

1 low-fat granola bar
Fruit Smoothie (see page 31)

Lunch

Veggie Sandwich
1 whole-wheat pita or tortilla
1–2 oz. cheese
3 slices of tomato
1 lettuce leaf

Recipe: FRUIT SMOOTHIE

DRINK FOR ENERGY!

Throw together a super-simple fruit smoothie for fast nutrition.

Ingredients:

Your favorite fruit, such as a banana, frozen blueberries, or strawberries
1/2 c. low-fat milk
1/2 c. low-fat vanilla yogurt
5 ice cubes
1 tbsp. honey (optional)
2 tsp. wheat germ (optional)

Put all the ingredients into a blender and blend until smooth.

5 cucumber slices
1 tsp. mustard
1/2 c. unsalted pretzels

Snack

1 apple, sliced
2 tbsp. peanut butter

Dinner

4 oz. broiled steak
1 baked potato
1/2 c. broccoli, cooked
1 whole-wheat roll

Today, lunch and dinner provide about 2 1/2 cups of vegetables. The granola bar, pita, pretzels, roll, and baked potato supply a steady stream of energy-producing complex carbohydrates. Also, we have covered our dairy needs with the yogurt smoothie for breakfast and cheddar cheese at lunch. The nuts in the granola bar, the peanut butter in our snack, and the steak at dinner will give us enough protein to keep our muscles strong.

Day 4

Rather than sweetening your waffles with syrup, which is high in sugar and calories, try topping them with fresh strawberries instead for a lighter and just as sweet and delicious breakfast.

Breakfast

2 whole-wheat waffles
1/2 c. sliced strawberries
1 c. skim milk

Lunch

1 c. mixed greens
2–3 oz. tuna, grilled
1/4 c. dried cranberries
1–2 oz. blue cheese, crumbled
1 tsp. balsamic vinaigrette

Snack

1/3 c. hummus
6 wheat crackers

Dinner

1 c. cooked spaghetti, with Vegetable Tomato Sauce (see page 33)

Dessert

1 Banana Pop (see page 33)

Recipe: VEGETABLE TOMATO SAUCE

Ingredients

1/4 c. chopped zucchini
1/4 c. yellow squash
2 tbsp. chopped onion
2 c. tomato sauce

Directions: Lightly stir-fry chopped zucchini, squash, and onions. Add to tomato sauce. Serve.

This menu starts off the day with 1 ounce of grains, 1/2 cup of fruit, and 1 cup of dairy at breakfast. Lunch allows us to hit several food groups—vegetables, fruits, dairy, and protein—in a tangy, tasty combination. New combinations of foods will keep your mouth happy and your body healthy. Hummus is a healthy and tasty change from higher-fat dips or

Recipe: BANANA POP

Ingredients

1 banana
1/2 c. low-fat vanilla yogurt
1/3 c. chopped peanuts or walnuts

Directions: The day before you want to have a cool treat, put a Popsicle stick in a banana. Dip the banana into yogurt and place the banana on a piece of wax paper. Sprinkle nuts on the yogurt-covered banana. Freeze.

cheeses. It can be spread on whole-grain crackers or pitas or provide a dip for raw vegetables. Hummus is made from chickpeas (also called garbanzo beans) and counts toward your ounces of protein for the day. Dinner provides 2 ounces of grains and over 2 cups of vegetables. Today we also have a fun dessert that adds fruit, dairy, and protein to our day's nutritional total.

Day 5

When beans and rice are eaten together, as in this burrito meal, they provide a low-fat version of the complete protein/amino acid combination found in animal proteins such as red meat, chicken, and fish.

Breakfast

1 whole-wheat bagel
2 tbsp. low-fat cream cheese
1 c. orange juice

Lunch

1 c. skim milk
Small side salad
1 tbsp. olive oil–and–vinegar dressing
Small baked potato
4 oz. Baked Chicken Nuggets (see page 35)

Snack

1/2 c. unsweetened applesauce

Dinner

Burritos
2 tortillas
1/4 c. refried beans

Recipe: BAKED CHICKEN NUGGETS

Foods that are normally high in fat are made much healthier by changing the way they are cooked. Here chicken nuggets are baked rather than fried for a nutritious and tasty lunch!

Ingredients

3/4 c. flour
1/2 tbsp. paprika
1/2 tsp. garlic powder
1/4 tsp. black pepper
3 4-oz. chicken breasts
1 tbsp. olive oil

Directions: Preheat oven to 350° Fahrenheit (177°C). Coat a 9-by-9-inch casserole dish with olive oil or nonstick spray. Mix flour and spices in large, sealable plastic bag. Cut chicken into two-inch (five-centimeter) nuggets. Dip nuggets into olive oil. Place in bag with flour and spices. Shake the bag until the chicken is coated. Place in casserole dish and cover with foil. Bake in oven for twenty minutes. Take foil off and flip nuggets. Bake for another ten minutes until chicken is completely white inside and brown on the outside. Makes about three servings.

1/2 c. brown rice, cooked
3 lettuce leaves, shredded
1 tomato, chopped
1 onion, chopped
1 green pepper, chopped
1 tbsp. plain yogurt
1/4 c. cheese, shredded

There are a variety of foods featured in today's menu. Five ounces of protein come from the chicken nuggets and beans. The bagel, rice, breading, and tortillas provide about 6 ounces of grain. Orange juice and applesauce take care of 1 1/2 cups of fruit. Milk, plain yogurt, and cheese contribute to the dairy needs. Also, the lunch salad and dinner veggies give us more than 3 cups of vegetables. Today's menu is well-balanced and delicious!

This five-day meal plan is a basic approach to the many different food choices you can make to create a healthy diet. Don't feel limited by these options and examples or obligated to repeat them over and over. Instead, take what you have learned in this book and experiment with creating meals on your own. There is no limit to the different dishes you can make when you use nutrient-rich ingredients.

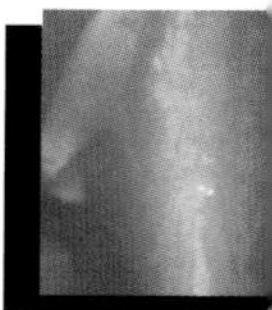
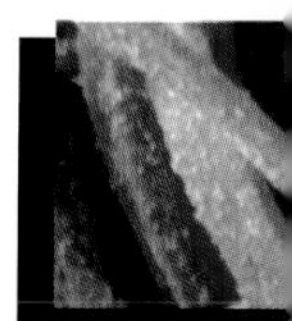
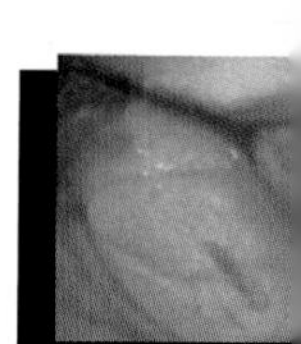

Conclusion

Creating and maintaining a healthy lifestyle does not have to be hard work. Take what you have learned about nutrition and food safety and apply it to your life. If your diet is not very healthy right now, start by taking little steps to improve it. Change little things at first, like not drinking soda as often or replacing your snack of cookies or potato chips with granola bars or trail mix. Build on these little steps, gradually removing the high-fat, sugary, and empty-calorie foods from your daily meals and replacing them with more whole grains, vegetables, and fruits.

In many households, it is parents who are in charge of planning and preparing the family's meals. Ask your parents if you can help plan and prepare the meals from now on. Look at the food you have in the kitchen and decide with your parents which foods could be put together to make healthy meals. Go shopping with them and help them make good choices about which foods to buy. Suggest baking, grilling, or steaming foods instead of frying foods or cooking them in butter. Experiment with different recipes and ingredients, and try nutritious alternatives to some of the more unhealthy foods you eat. Getting involved in meal preparation will help make you more

Planning, shopping, and cooking together can be a great way for you and your family to create more nutritious meals and support each other in developing eating habits that will lead to longer and healthier lives.

aware of what you are putting into your body and keep you and your family healthy. Your parents will appreciate the help with cooking, shopping, and planning, and everyone in your family will benefit from the nutritious meals.

Eating well, along with regular exercise, is a major part of living a healthier lifestyle. The benefits of good nutrition will stay with you for the rest of your long and healthy life. A healthy diet will help you look and feel great. Your body will remain stronger later in life, and you will be less likely to be affected by serious illnesses. Planning and preparing balanced meals today will improve your health right now and for years to come.

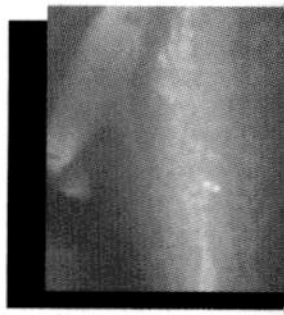

Glossary

anorexia nervosa An eating disorder characterized by a fear of gaining weight, which leads to not eating or eating very little.

bacteria Microscopic, single-celled organisms.

bulimia nervosa An eating disorder in which the person who is affected eats an enormous amount of food and then vomits or takes laxatives to force his or her body to expel the food before it can be digested.

calcium A mineral important to the makeup of most plants and animals. In humans and animals, it helps build and strengthen bones and teeth, and regulate muscle contractions.

calorie A unit of measure that indicates how much energy a food will provide.

carbohydrate A nutrient that provides the human body with the energy it needs to function. Carbohydrates are found in grains, starches, milk products, fruits, vegetables, and sweets.

cholesterol A substance found in animal tissues and some foods (such as red meat and eggs) that is used in building cell tissues. In humans, it can build up in the arteries, causing dangerous blockages.

fiber Coarse, indigestible plant matter.

foodborne illness A sickness that is transferred to people through contaminated food.

minerals Inorganic substances found in nature and vital to the nutrition of plants and animals, including humans.

monounsaturated fat An oil or fatty acid that may reduce the levels of harmful blood cholesterol.

nutrition The processes by which an individual takes in and utilizes food material.

polyunsaturated fat An oil or fatty acid that may help reduce harmful blood cholesterol levels.

protein A nutrient found in meats, beans, nuts, and some other foods that is responsible for repairing and building cells in the body.

salmonella A bacteria that causes food poisoning in humans.

saturated fat A fat or fatty acid that is solid at room temperature and has been linked to an increased risk of coronary heart disease.

trans fat An unhealthy substance that is made when food manufacturers turn liquid oils into solid fats by adding hydrogen (in a process called hydrogenation). Trans fat can be found in vegetable shortenings, some margarines, crackers, cookies, snack foods, and other foods made with or fried in partially hydrogenated oils.

vitamins Any of a group of organic substances essential to the nutrition of most animals and some plants. They are present in food and sometimes produced in the body. They do not provide energy, but they are necessary for many bodily functions.

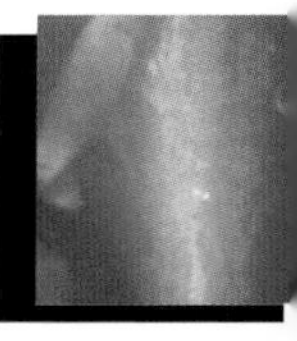

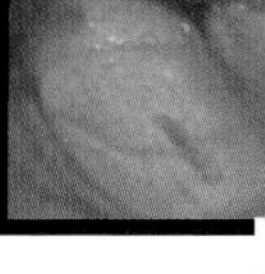

For More Information

The American Dietetic Association
120 South Riverside Plaza, Suite 2000
Chicago, IL 60606-6995
(800) 877-1600
Web site: http://www.eatright.org

American Public Health Association
800 I Street NW
Washington, DC 20001
(202) 777-2742
Web site: http://www.apha.org

Food and Drug Administration
5600 Fishers Lane
Rockville, MD 20857
(888) 463-6332
Web site: http://www.fda.gov

Food and Nutrition Information Center
Agricultural Research Service, USDA
National Agricultural Library, Room 105
10301 Baltimore Avenue
Beltsville, MD 20705-2351
(301) 504-5719
Web site: http://www.nal.usda.gov/fnic

National Institutes of Health (NIH)
9000 Rockville Pike
Bethesda, MD 20892
(301) 496-4000
Web site: http://www.nih.gov

U.S. Department of Agriculture (USDA)
Center for Nutrition Policy and Promotion
3101 Park Center Drive, Room 1034
Alexandria, VA 22302
(888) 779-7264
Web site: http://www.mypyramid.gov

U.S. Food and Drug Administration (FDA)
Center for Food Safety and Applied Nutrition
5600 Fishers Lane
Rockville, MD 20857
(888) INFO-FDA
Web site: http://vm.cfsan.fda.gov/list.html

Web Sites

Due to the changing nature of Internet links, the Rosen Publishing Group, Inc., has developed an online list of Web sites related to the subject of this book. This site is updated regularly. Please use this link to access the list:

http://www.rosenlinks.com/linu/pphms

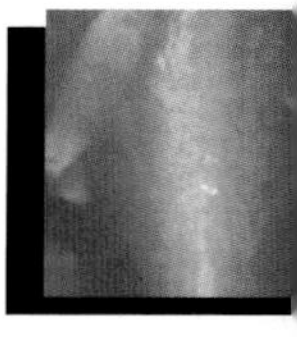

For Further Reading

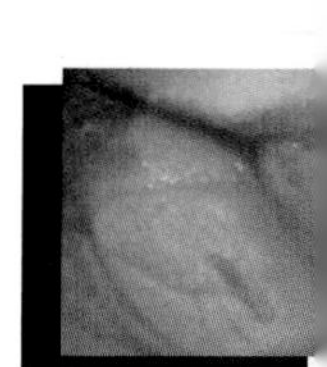

Braman, Arlette N. *Kids Around the World Cook!* New York: John Wiley and Sons, 2000.

Collison, Cathey, and Janis Campbell, eds. *Heart Smart Kids Cookbook.* Detroit, MI: Detroit Free Press, 2000.

D'Amico, Joan, and Karen Eich Drummond. *The Healthy Body Cookbook: Over 50 Fun Activities and Delicious Recipes for Kids.* New York: John Wiley and Sons, 1998.

Kalman, Bobbie. *Breakfast Blast.* New York: Crabtree Publishers, 2003.

King, Hazel. *Carbohydrates for a Healthy Body.* Chicago, IL: Heinemann Library, 2003.

Nissenberg, Sandra K. *The Healthy Start Kids' Cookbook: Fun and Healthful Recipes That Kids Can Make Themselves.* New York: John Wiley and Sons, 1998.

Rockwell, Lizzy. *Good Enough to Eat: A Kid's Guide to Food and Nutrition.* New York: HarperCollins Publishers, 1999.

Salter, Charles A. *The Nutrition-Fitness Link: How Diet Can Help Your Body and Mind.* Brookfield, CT: Millbrook Press, 1993.

Warner, Penny. *Healthy Treats and Super Snacks for Kids.* New York: McGraw Hill Companies, 1994.

Wilkes, Angela. *Children's Quick and Easy Cookbook.* New York: DK Publishing, 1997.

Bibliography

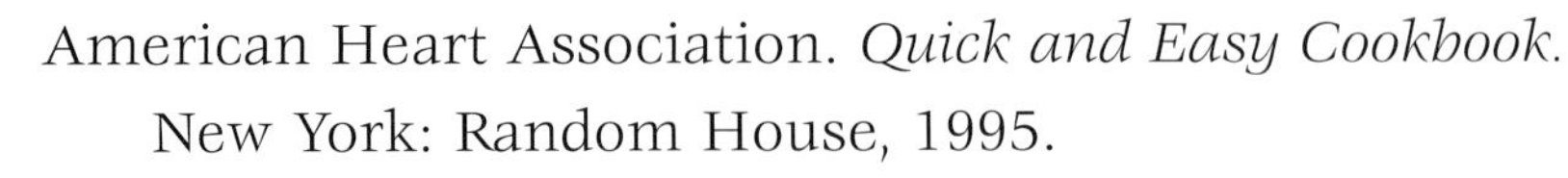

American Heart Association. *Quick and Easy Cookbook.* New York: Random House, 1995.

"Breakfast Cereal May Help Children Promote Healthy Body Weight." American Dietetic Association, 2004. Retrieved March 2004 (http://www.eatright.org/Public/NutritionInformation/index_18506.cfm).

"Consumer Information on the New Trans Fat Labeling Requirements." U.S. FDA's Center for Food Safety and Applied Nutrition, March 2004. Retrieved April 2004 (http://vm.cfsan.fda.gov/~dms/transfat.html).

Dietz, William H., and Loraine Stern, eds. *American Academy of Pediatrics: Guide to Your Child's Nutrition.* New York: Random House, 1999.

Drayer, Lisa. "Diet, Nutrition, and Weight Management." CNN Access, August 2001. Retrieved March 2004 (http://www.cnn.com/2001/Community/08/22/drayer.cnna).

Duyff, Roberta Larson. *The American Dietetic Association's Complete Food and Nutrition Guide.* Minneapolis, MN: Chronimed Publishing, 1998.

"Figuring Out Food Labels" KidsHealth.org, August 2003. Retrieved April 2004 (http://kidshealth.org/kid/stay_healthy/food/labels.html).

Kaehler, Kathy. *Teenage Fitness: Get Fit, Look Great, Feel Great!* New York: Cliff Street Books, 2001.

"MyPyramid.gov: Steps to a Healthier You." USDA. Retrieved November 2007 (http://www.mypyramid.gov).

Papazian, Ruth. "On the Teen Scene: Should You Go on a Diet." *FDA Consumer Magazine*, September 1993. Retrieved March 2004 (http://www.fda.gov/fdac/reprints/ots_diet.html).

U.S. Food and Drug Administration. "Teen Science Classes Serve Up Lessons in Food Safety." *FDA Consumer Magazine*, Jan–Feb 2002. Retrieved March 2004 (http://www.fda.gov/fdac/features/2002/102_teen.html).

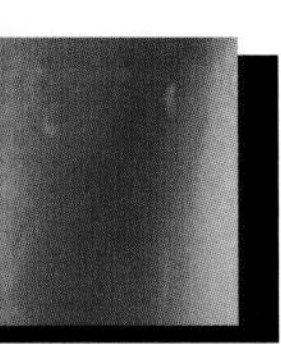
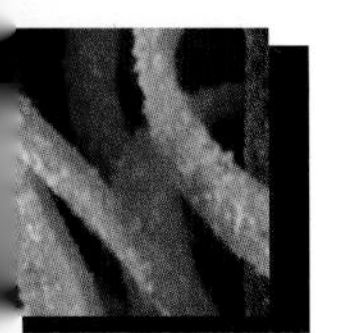
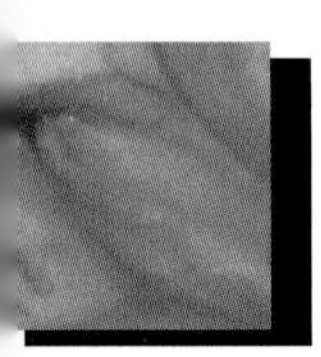

Index

About the Author

Jennifer Silate has written more than 100 books for children. She currently lives in Maryland.

Photo Credits

Cover (background images), back cover images, title page (background images), pp. 3, 4, 7, 15, 21, 26, 37, 39, 41, 43, 44 © David Wasserman/ Artville; cover image, title page image © Michael Keller/Corbis; p. 5 © Mark Peterson/Corbis; p. 6 © Howard Kingsnorth/Getty Images; p. 8 courtesy of MyPyramid.gov; p. 10 photo by Scott Bauer/Agricultural Research Service/United States Department of Agriculture; p. 13 © Lester V. Bergman/Corbis; pp. 14, 19 © AP/World Wide Photos; p. 16 courtesy of the Food and Drug Administration; p. 18 © Layne Kennedy/Corbis; p. 20 © Michelle Garrett/ Corbis; p. 22 © Image Source Limited/Index Stock Imagery; p. 23 © SW Productions/Getty Images; p. 24 © Ted Horowitz/ Corbis; p. 27 © The Image Works Archive; pp. 28, 29, 33 (bottom) © Stockfood; p. 31 © Royalty-Free/Corbis; p. 32 © Robin MacDougall/ Getty Images; pp. 33 (top), 34, 35 © Japack Company/Corbis; p. 38 © Ariel Skelley/Corbis.

Designer: Geri Fletcher; **Editor:** John Kemmerer